Manners

Manners at the Library

by Terri DeGezelle

Consultant:
Madonna Murphy, PhD, Professor of Education
University of St. Francis, Joliet, Illinois
Author, *Character Education in America's Blue Ribbon Schools*

Capstone
press

Mankato, Minnesota

First Facts is published by Capstone Press
151 Good Counsel Drive, P.O. Box 669, Mankato, Minnesota 56002
www.capstonepress.com

Library of Congress Cataloging-in-Publication Data
DeGezelle, Terri, 1955–
    Manners at the library / by Terri DeGezelle.
       p. cm.—(First facts. Manners)
    Includes bibliographical references and index.
    Contents: A trip to the library—Being polite—Showing respect—Showing courtesy
Sharing—Being helpful—Being patient—Good manners—Amazing but true!—Hands
on: bookmarks.
    ISBN 0-7368-2645-9 (hardcover)
    1. Library etiquette—Juvenile literature. 2. Etiquette for children and teenagers. [1. Etiquette.
2. Behavior. 3. Libraries.] I. Title. II. Series.
Z716.43.D43 2005
027—dc22   2003024468

Editorial Credits
Christine Peterson, editor; Juliette Peters, designer; Wanda Winch, photo researcher; Eric Kudalis,
    product planning editor

Photo Credits
Capstone Press/Gary Sundermeyer, cover (background)
Capstone Press/Gem Photo Studio/Dan Delaney, cover (foreground), 4–5, 6, 7, 8, 9, 10–11, 12, 13,
    14–15, 16, 17, 18–19
Folio Inc./Robert C. Shafer, 20

Artistic Effects
Capstone Press/Juliette Peters, 21

1 2 3 4 5 6 09 08 07 06 05 04

Table of Contents

A Trip to the Library

People enjoy visiting the library. Good **manners** help everyone have fun. People with good manners are kind and **polite** to others. Alec and Carlee practice good manners when they visit the library.

Fun Fact!

In the United States, more people visit libraries than go to movies.

Being Polite

The library is a quiet place. Polite people do not bother others. They use quiet voices to read out loud.

Being polite also means being nice to others. A friend helps Alec find a book. Alec remembers to say "please" and "thank you."

Showing Respect

People show **respect** when they follow the library's rules. People return books on time. They do not eat or drink in the library.

People also can show respect for library books. They write on paper instead of library books. People keep books clean. They keep the pages flat.

Showing Courtesy

People show **courtesy** when they use good manners with others. Kids can show courtesy when the **librarian** reads a book. Boys and girls listen quietly to the story. They raise their hands before speaking.

Fun Fact!
The United States has more public libraries than McDonald's restaurants.

11

Sharing

People share at the library by taking turns. They share books, newspapers, and magazines. Carlee and Alec share books they both need for homework.

Everyone shares the library's computers. People take turns looking up information. When Carlee's turn is over, she lets a friend use the computer.

Being Helpful

Librarians are helpful people. They teach people how to find information. Librarians help people look for books on the shelves. They help people use computers. Polite people thank librarians for their help.

Fun Fact!
About 137,000 librarians work in U.S. libraries.

Being Patient

People check out library books before taking them home. **Patient** people wait quietly in line. Carlee is patient as she waits to check out her books.

At her turn, Carlee hands her library card to the librarian. The librarian **scans** the card and books. Carlee waits patiently for her books.

Good Manners

Alec and Carlee used good manners at the library. They used quiet voices when talking. They politely asked the librarian for help. They will take care of their library books. It's fun to visit the library when everyone uses good manners.

Fun Fact!
In the United States, most people check out at least seven library books a year.

The Library of Congress in Washington, D.C., is the largest library in the world. The library opened in 1800. The library has almost 530 miles (850 kilometers) of shelves. It has nearly 19 million books, 12 million photographs, and 5 million maps.

Hands On: Bookmarks

Bookmarks save your place when you read a book. You can also use a bookmark to help remember library manners. Have an adult help you make a bookmark.

What You Need

scissors
construction paper
markers or crayons
black marker

What You Do

1. With an adult's help, cut a piece of construction paper that is 6 inches (15 centimeters) long and 4 inches (10 centimeters) wide.
2. Use markers or crayons to decorate your bookmark.
3. With a black marker, write a good manner or library rule on the bookmark. Some ideas are listed below.
   - Remember to use a quiet voice at the library.
   - Treat library books like friends.
   - Return all library books on time.
4. Use your bookmark to keep your place in a library book.

Glossary

courtesy (KUR-tuh-see)—behaving in a way that shows good behavior toward others

librarian (lye-BRER-ee-uhn)—someone who works in a library; librarians organize books and other materials.

manners (MAN-urss)—polite behavior

patient (PAY-shuhnt)—able to wait quietly without getting angry or upset

polite (puh-LITE)—having good manners; polite people are kind and respectful.

respect (ri-SPEKT)—the belief in the quality and worth of others, yourself, and your surroundings

scan (SKAN)—to move a beam of light over an object to get information

Read More

Monroe, Judy. *A Day in the Life of a Librarian.* First Facts. Community Helpers at Work. Mankato, Minn.: Capstone Press, 2005.

Nelson, Robin. *Following Rules.* First Step NonFiction. Minneapolis: Lerner, 2003.

Internet Sites

FactHound offers a safe, fun way to find Internet sites related to this book. All of the sites on FactHound have been researched by our staff.

Here's how:
1. Visit *www.facthound.com*
2. Type in this special code **0736826459** for age-appropriate sites. Or enter a search word related to this book for a more general search.
3. Click on the **Fetch It** button.

FactHound will fetch the best sites for you!

Index